AF228354

Read for a
Better World™

MONSTER TRUCKS

A First Look

PERCY LEED

GRL Consultant, Diane Craig, Certified Literacy Specialist

Lerner Publications ◆ Minneapolis

Educator Toolbox

Reading books is a great way for kids to express what they're interested in. Before reading this title, ask the reader these questions:

What do you think this book is about? Look at the cover for clues.

What do you already know about monster trucks?

What do you want to learn about monster trucks?

Let's Read Together

Encourage the reader to use the pictures to understand the text.

Point out when the reader successfully sounds out a word.

Praise the reader for recognizing sight words such as *is* and *the*.

TABLE OF CONTENTS

Monster Trucks

Monster trucks are very large trucks.

www.swampthing4x4.co.uk
7
SWAMP THING
Ford
LUCAS OIL
0808 100 3259 • www.LucasOil.co.u
RAMIREN
EHITUSSEADMETE RENT JA MÜ
5

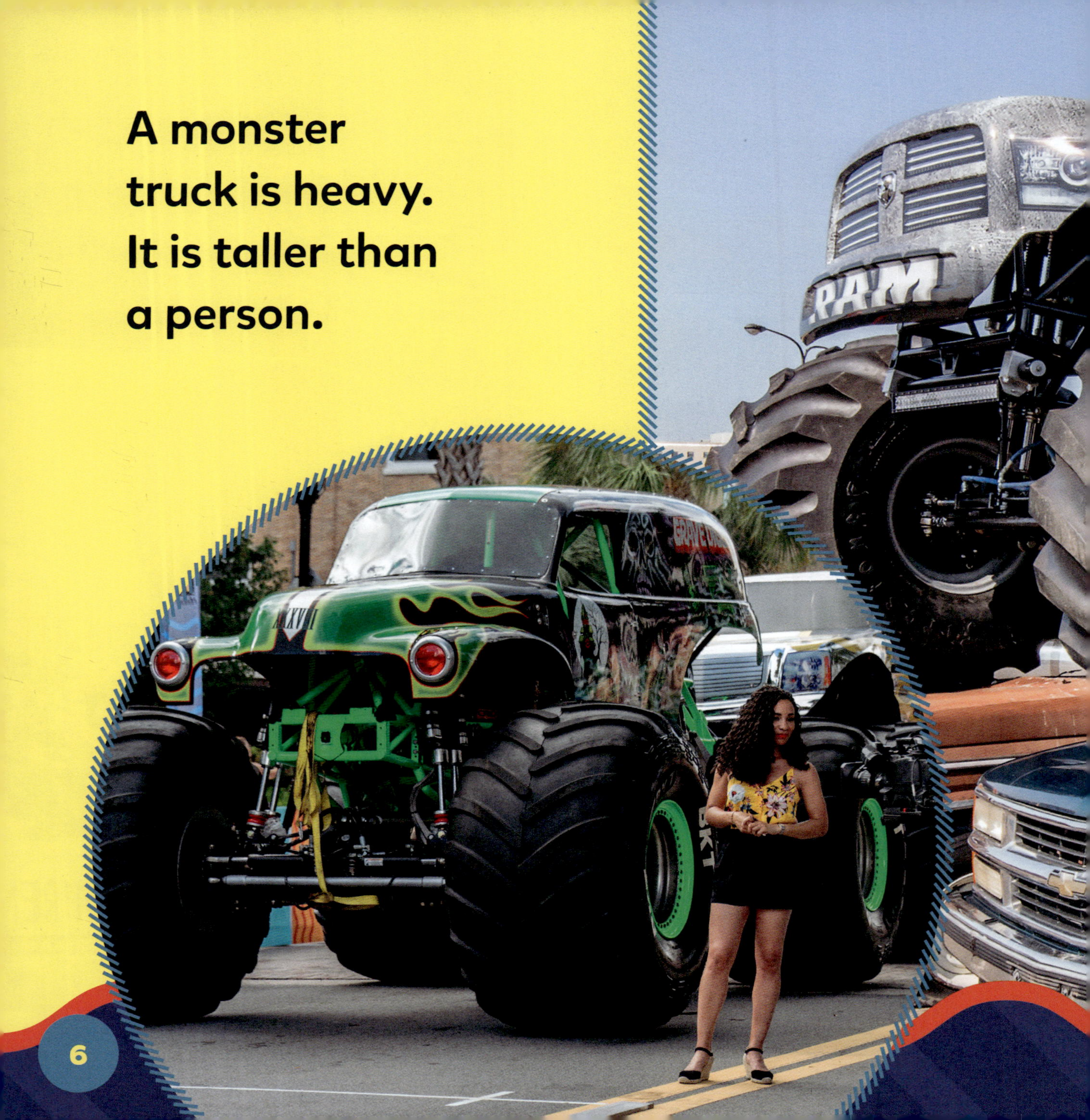

A monster
truck is heavy.
It is taller than
a person.

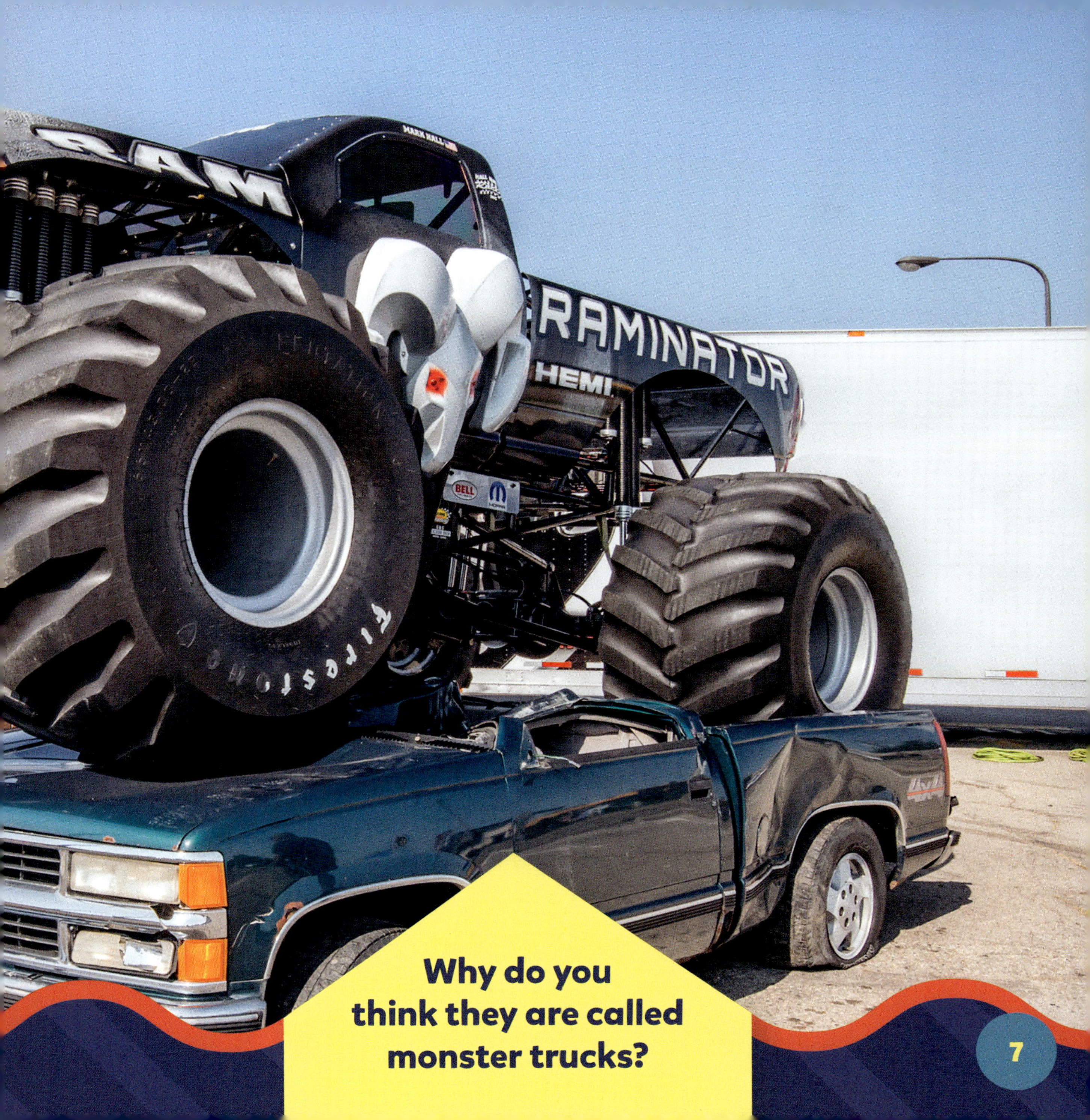
Why do you
think they are called
monster trucks?

Monster trucks have
four big tires.

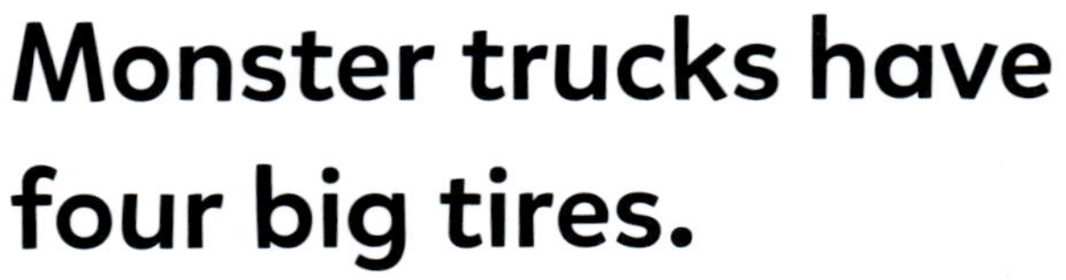

8

They can drive on one wheel.

cage
01

Monster trucks
have cages.
They keep
the driver safe.

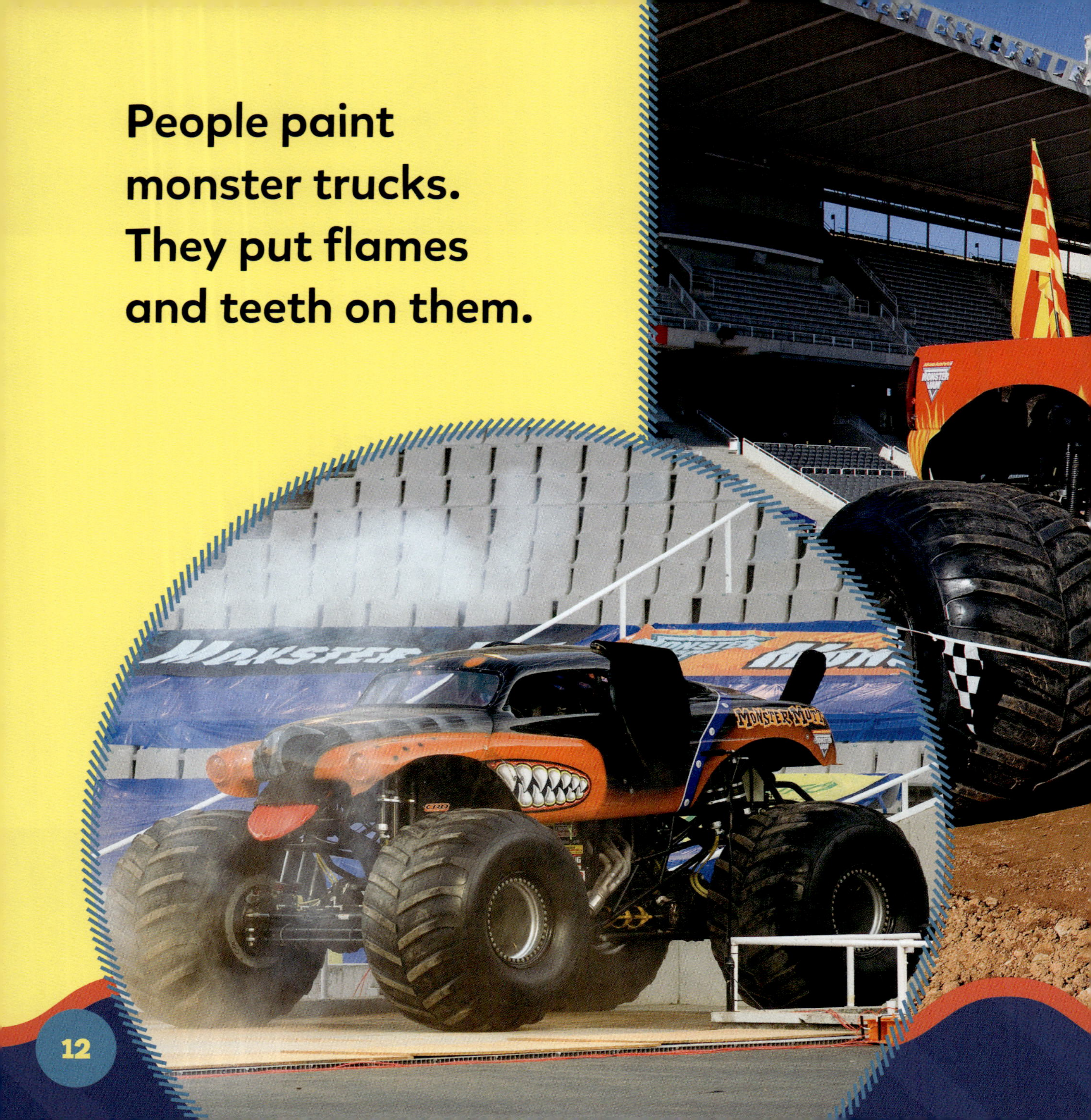

People paint
monster trucks.
They put flames
and teeth on them.

12

13

Allianz (iii) Parque
WTORRE
MONSTER JAM
Allianz Parque
Allianz Seguros

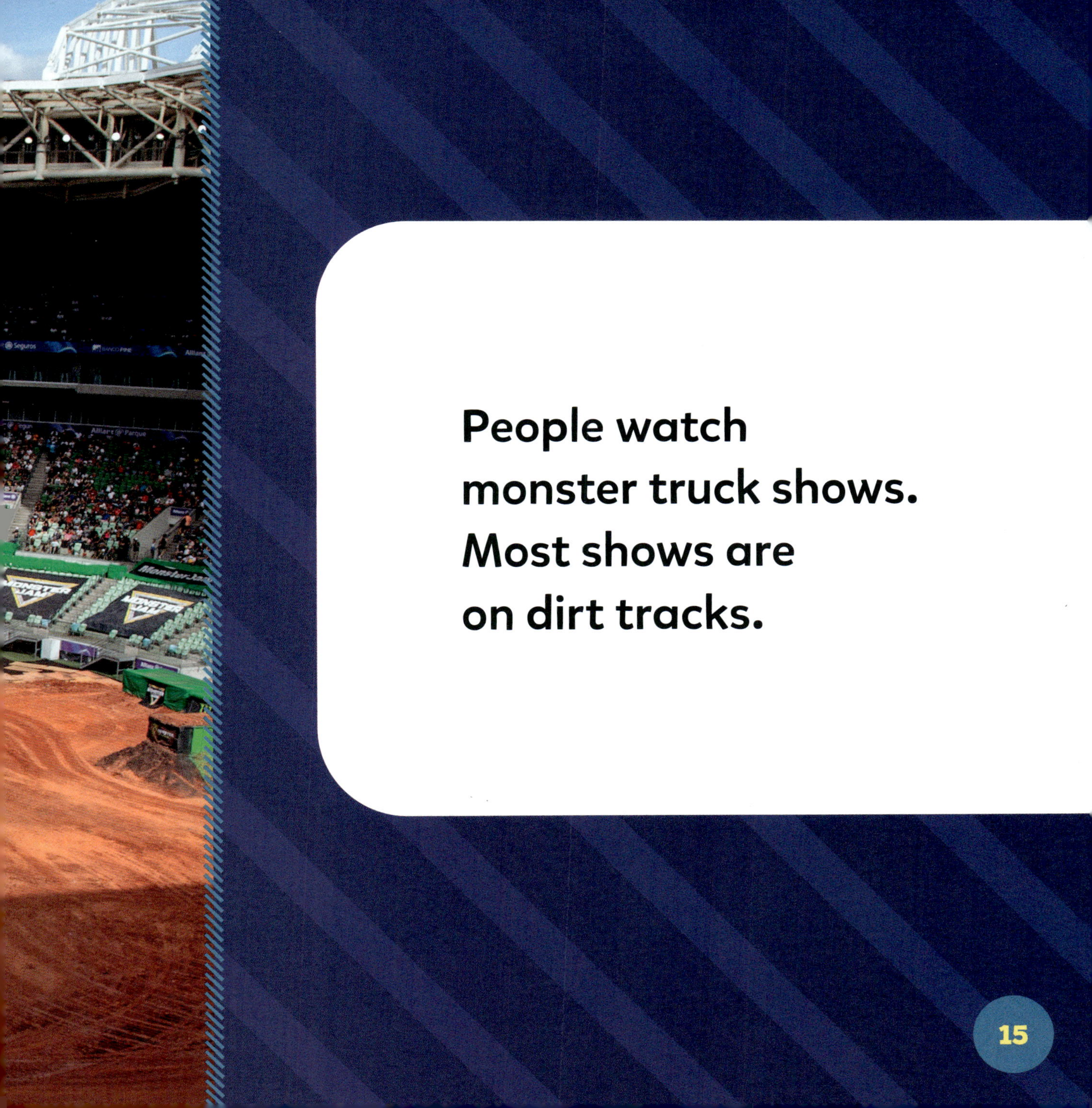

People watch
monster truck shows.
Most shows are
on dirt tracks.

There are hills and jumps.
Monster trucks do tricks.
They can do flips.

16

BKT
BKT
GRAVE DIGGER
PREVENTURA

Trucks drive
over cars.
Two trucks race.

Why can
monster trucks drive
over cars?

Monster truck shows are loud.
They are fun to watch.

You Connect!

Have you ever seen a monster truck?

Would you want to drive
a monster truck?

How can you learn more
about monster trucks?

STEM Snapshot

Encourage students to think and ask questions like scientists. Ask the reader:

What is something you learned about monster trucks?

What is something you noticed about monster truck parts?

What is something you still want to learn about monster trucks?

Photo Glossary

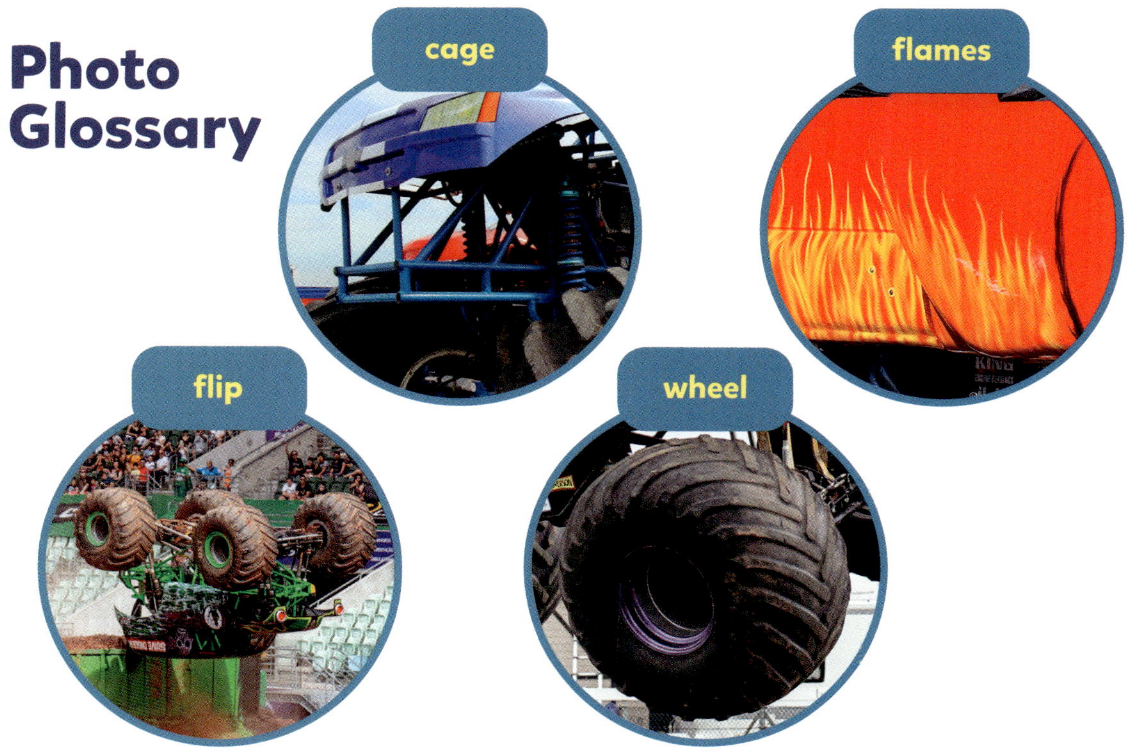

Learn More

Arnold, Tedd. *Fly Guy Presents: Monster Trucks*. New York: Scholastic, 2019.

Fishman, Jon M. *Cool Pickup Trucks*. Minneapolis: Lerner Publications, 2019.

McDonald, Amy. *Monster Trucks*. Minneapolis: Bellwether Media, 2021.

Index

cages, 11

paint, 12, 13

race, 18

shows, 15, 20

tires, 8

tricks, 16

wheel, 9

Photo Acknowledgments

The images in this book are used with the permission of: © Maksim Shmeljov/Shutterstock Images, pp. 4–5; © semyon lorberg/Shutterstock Images, p. 6; © Steve Lagreca/Shutterstock Images, pp. 6–7; © Simon Bratt/Shutterstock Images, pp. 8, 23 (wheel); © BW Press/Shutterstock Images, pp. 9, 14–15, 16 (inset), 16–17, 18–19, 20, 23 (flip); © Photomarine/Shutterstock Images, pp. 10–11, 23 (cage); © Natursports/Shutterstock Images, pp. 12 (inset), 12–13, 23 (flames); © Dan Hanscom/Shutterstock Images, p. 18.

Cover Photograph: © BW Press/Shutterstock Images

Design Elements: © Mighty Media, Inc.

Lerner Publications Company
An imprint of Lerner Publishing Group, Inc.
241 First Avenue North
Minneapolis, MN 55401 USA

For reading levels and more information, look up this title at www.lernerbooks.com.

Main body text set in Mikado a Medium.
Typeface provided by Hannes von Doehren.

Library of Congress Cataloging-in-Publication Data

Names: Leed, Percy, 1968–author.
Title: Monster trucks : a first look / Percy Leed.
Description: Minneapolis : Lerner Publications, [2024] | Series: Read about vehicles (Read for a better world) | Includes bibliographical references and index. | Audience: Ages 5-8 | Audience: Grades K–1 | Summary: "Monster trucks are loud and monstrous. People go to shows to see the painted cars flip in the air. Carefully leveled text and full-color photographs help these vehicles jump off the page"—Provided by publisher.
Identifiers: LCCN 2022034680 (print) | LCCN 2022034681 (ebook) | ISBN 9781728491455 (library binding) | ISBN 9798765603642 (paperback) ISBN 9781728499901 (ebook)
Subjects: LCSH: Monster trucks—Juvenile literature.
Classification: LCC TL230.5.M58 L44 2023 (print) | LCC TL230.5.M58 (ebook) | DDC 629.223/2—dc23/eng/20221223

LC record available at https://lccn.loc.gov/2022034680
LC ebook record available at https://lccn.loc.gov/2022034681

Manufactured in the United States of America
1 - CG - 7/15/23